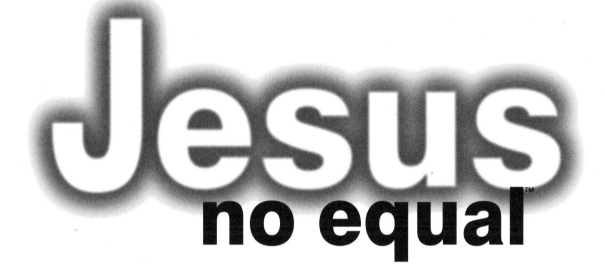

Jesus
no equal™

a passionate encounter with the Son of God

leader's guide

Dedication

To Carol and Laurene, our faithful wives, who recently left this
world and now behold Jesus in all His unequaled majesty.

Acknowledgments

Special thanks to Dale Reeves, whose oversight and editorial
advice kept us on track and to Stuart Hall, for his creative input.

Most importantly, praise to Jesus, to whom belongs all the glory. Without Him we can do nothing.

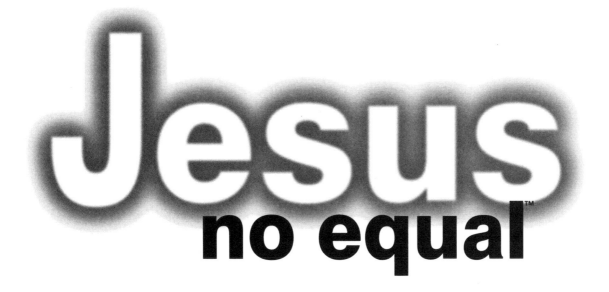

a passionate encounter with the Son of God

Barry St. Clair
Steve Miller

leader's guide

EMPOWERED™ Youth Products
Standard Publishing
Cincinnati, Ohio

Edited by Dale Reeves and Leslie Durden
Cover and inside design by Dina Sorn

Standard Publishing, Cincinnati, Ohio.
A division of Standex International Corporation.

06   05   04   03   02   01   00

5   4   3   2

ISBN: 0-7847-1042-2

Contents

Foreword

"Who is Jesus Christ? Can He *really* affect my life today?" In his book, *Jesus no equal*, Barry St. Clair addresses these questions head-on with experience, sincerity and a dose of humor. This book shows how our relationship with the Son of God affects all areas of our lives. If you are ready to be challenged by the radical life of Jesus, then this book is for you!

Jesus no equal traces Christ's coming: His birth, life, ministry, death and resurrection, then shows the role He desires to play in our lives today. Can we really trust Jesus with our dating life? Can we trust Him with our relationship with our parents? Will He truly guide my life in this century? Can He use me to impact my generation? This book helps us to honor and love Jesus more and then gives us specific and practical ways to do that.

In a world that encourages compromise and mediocrity, we must be equipped to make a difference. *Jesus no equal* gives us the tools we need to stand strong. Barry has created a unique blend of how Jesus not only satisfies the heart, but also the mind. It has truly hit the mark on what it means to be a disciple of Jesus in the twenty-first century!

Josh and Sean McDowell,
Josh McDowell Ministries

As I ran around the toddler room with a little car in my hand, I spotted another boy who looked a lot like me. I waddled over to say "Hi!" I don't remember ever shaking his hand, but I do remember his name . . . Bryan Clark. When my mom picked me up, all I could talk about was my new friend. Little did I know that Bryan would become my best friend through high school. Other friends have come along but none of them could fill the friendship that Bryan and I have shared. He has always been my best friend.

We all have stories like this one . . . stories of how we have found a friend who is always there for us, someone we can see and touch. Remember how it was when you found a girl or guy you really liked? You got a smile on your face just thinking about that special someone. Guys, remember how you talked about the girl to all your buddies in the locker room? Girls, remember how you giggled with your friends about how cute he was? Then, the big moment finally arrived. You got to talk to the person and you felt those huge butterflies in your stomach. It seemed as if you were floating and you couldn't come down. That's exactly how it should be in your relationship with Jesus.

I am one of the student leaders of *Revival Generation*—a movement that encourages teenagers to be bold in their faith on campus, praying for revival to come. We are a generation of teens falling in love with Jesus, a generation that considers Jesus their best friend, a generation that is experiencing revival, one heart at a time.

Barry St. Clair, even though he is not a teenager, is a student at heart. I have known Barry for a few years and have seen firsthand his great passion for Jesus. He has made me want to know Jesus more deeply. Barry is a man who knows what it means to love God. He has experienced the ultimate friendship with the Savior. In this book, Barry invites you to take the ultimate road trip to discover a friend who is closer than a brother. I pray that you will find Jesus in a way that many in our generation have. It takes faith to fall in love with someone you cannot physically see or touch, but if you are willing to take the risk, Jesus Christ will become your best friend.

I am convinced of this one thing: There is something very different about my generation. We know what it means to be hurt. We have gone through tragedies such as Columbine and Paducah. The world is asking how we will make it. The only answer I have is Jesus. This book is a tool to help you fall more in love with Him.

Josh Weidmann, student leader
Revival Generation, Littleton, CO

There is no equal to Jesus—not even a close second. And the more clearly we see the great chasm that separates Jesus from everything else that competes for our allegiance, the easier it is to submit to His lordship over every aspect of our personal lives. **The purpose of this study is to lead students to know Jesus more intimately and follow Him more passionately.** Our desire is that this leader's guide will help you achieve that purpose.

How the Materials Fit Together

For the greatest impact, use all four of the primary *Jesus no equal* resources. We have a book, devotionals at the end of each chapter, this leader's guide and two recommended CDs. Here's how they work together:

During the week prior to each session, have students read the corresponding chapter in the book *Jesus no equal*, by Barry St. Clair.

Also, before the meeting, students should try to complete five of the seven personal devotions. Although the material is designed for high-school students, you can tailor it to either college students or middle-school students. Middle-school students may wish to go through one-third or one-half of a devotional each day. A high-school student should be able to complete a devotional in 20-30 minutes.

This leader's guide is designed to help you direct students' learning. You get six complete studies, filled with illustrations, discussions and more ideas than you can use in one session. It does not duplicate the material presented in either the book or devotional, but takes a new angle on each basic theme.

This study features songs from the *Listen: Louder* CD, a Sparrow Records compilation that delivers some powerful songs in the styles youth love. Each session in this book includes a song from one of today's favorite Christian artists that reinforces the theme of each session. Music is a powerful way to impact your students. If you don't already own a copy of the *Passion: Better Is One Day* CD, get one so that you can set a worshipful atmosphere before and after sessions. See the ordering information on page 48 of this book. Many students will want their own copy to enhance their personal worship. Check out your local Christian bookstore or go to www.passionnow.org or www.starsong.com.

You can use these resources in several settings:

Youth Group: Teach the material from the leader's guide during your weekly youth meetings. We include ideas for the large group setting.

Summer Camp: The six sessions are designed to be your camp program.

Small Groups: Provide your students the opportunity to meet in small groups to discuss their discoveries from the book. Use the study to make disciples and build leaders by using parents and college students to lead the groups. The leader's guide should provide everything they need to lead groups effectively.

1-2-1: Challenge your students to invite one non-Christian friend to meet together over the summer to go through the book together. See pages 175, 176 of the *Jesus no equal* book for some ideas that will encourage your students to be missionaries to their friends and their school.

Campus Ministry: The materials are designed so that either students or adults can lead groups through this study in campus club meetings. If students used just one devotional from the book per week, they would have enough material for a whole year in a campus club!

We provide enough material for you to customize it according to your needs. **Student-led groups and small groups** may want to skip some of the large-group activities (although some could work equally well in small groups) and concentrate on the discussion questions.

Discipleship groups (and those with a higher level of commitment) could challenge students to complete all the devotions, while **lower commitment groups** may challenge students to complete four or five devotions per week.

If you need to order additional copies of the *Jesus no equal* devotional, check out your local Christian bookstore or visit www.standardpub.com.

Groups with access to media will want to plan ahead to secure videos and order CDs. The United States Copyright Act treats displays or performance of multimedia presentations, films and videotapes by nonprofit organizations (including churches) to a small group of individuals as "public performances" even if no admission fee is charged. The fact that the church or one of its members may have purchased the copy of the film or videotape makes no difference. To avoid running afoul of the "public performance" prohibition in the Copyright Act, you must in each instance secure the copyright owner's permission or alternatively obtain an "umbrella license" from the Motion Picture Licensing Corporation. To learn more about the umbrella license, contact the MPLC at 1-800-462-8855 or visit them on the web at www.mplc.com. You may also want to visit http://fairuse.stanford.edu/ for additional information on the Copyright Act and the "Fair Use Doctrine."

Hints for Leaders

1. Plan Ahead

Six Weeks in Advance

Begin building expectation for the upcoming series. Purchase the *Passion: Better Is One Day* CD and *Listen: Louder* CD so you can familiarize yourself with the songs. Start playing songs along with your announcements of the upcoming series. Then, turn down the volume as you challenge students to purchase the *Jesus no equal* book. (If students pay for the book, they will take the challenge more seriously.)

Four Weeks in Advance

Order enough *Jesus no equal* books for your students and leaders. Order enough leader's guides and CDs for each leader. Read through the sessions well in advance, so that you can plan ahead to rent videos for needed clips or allow students time to prepare for their involvement in certain sessions. After reading through all the sessions, consider watching the *Jesus* film and choose clips that fit best with each section. (His birth, death and resurrection are no-brainers.) The movie can be ordered for $14.95 at http://www.jesusfilm.org/.

Session three recommends that you follow up with some type of service event to give students the opportunity to live out the lesson. Begin now to plan a visit to a nursing home, shut-ins, etc.

Session four includes a presentation of the gospel. Your denomination may recommend a booklet that includes your special denominational emphasis. If possible, plan to use some kind of booklet that presents the steps to salvation. The advantages of this tool are these:
- Students can take the booklet home and reflect more deeply on their decision.
- They can sign their name and record the date on the back of the booklet, giving them a way to dispel future doubts by having a record of exactly what decision they made.
- Students can take extra copies to share with their friends.

Whichever way you choose to present the gospel, you'll want to have pencils and printed decision cards available for this session.

2. Get the Bigger Picture

The Challenge 2000 Covenant, which you will find on page 9, has been signed by thousands of students around the country. One of our main goals in this series is to ready the hearts of our students to sign this covenant, thereby uniting them with a significant movement of students and adult leaders nationwide who have committed themselves to communicate the gospel of Jesus Christ to every teenager. To prepare students for this challenge, make the Covenant a visual part of each session. Put it on an overhead or a large poster and refer to it at the beginning of each session by saying, "This covenant has been signed by thousands of students across the country. By the end of this series, I hope that you will be willing to sign the covenant and then live it."

CHALLENGE 2000 COVENANT

Because Jesus loves me and I love Him, I will:

Commit

myself to a love relationship with Jesus Christ—through praying, studying His Word, and allowing His Spirit to lead me each day.

—Matthew 22:36-38

Honor

Christ in my moral life—my thoughts, words, actions and relationships.

—1 Timothy 4:12

Respect

my parents and all authorities in my life—with love, honor and obedience.

—Ephesians 6:1-3; Romans 13:1

Involve

myself in encouraging and uniting with other Christians—regardless of race, church or social status.

—Hebrews 10:24, 25

Seek

God through prayer—asking Him daily to bring spiritual awakening to my generation.

—2 Chronicles 7:14

Take

the message of Christ to my school and world—by praying, living and witnessing so that every student has an opportunity to know Christ.

—Acts 1:8

Believing God has a special destiny and mission for me and my generation, I take this challenge, relying on the Holy Spirit.

I join young people and youth workers across our country to pray for a spiritual awakening, and to help take the message of Christ to every school and every young person by year-end 2000.

_____   _____
Signed   Date

The Students' Creed, which you will find at the beginning of each session, gives a thumbnail sketch of some beliefs that unite believers. Creeds have been significant historically to clarify important truths and guard against heresy. Put it on an overhead and repeat it in unison with your students each week, emphasizing the portion that comes out of the current lesson.

Students' Creed

JESUS CHRIST:

REVEALED UNIQUELY

BORN A VIRGIN BIRTH

LIVED A SINLESS LIFE

DIED A SINNER'S DEATH

RAISED FROM THE DEAD

RETURNING TO RULE

3. Be Authentic

Often, the most important ingredient in a life-changing message is that the teacher is being transformed by the message. A youth ministry hero of mine used to say, "If you want your youth to bleed, you've got to hemorrhage!" In that light, applying these messages to our own lives as leaders is our first priority.

"But I'm just not there," some of you may object. "I know Him, but not intimately. I follow Him, but I'm not sure how passionate I am about it. How can I guide them to a place I've never been?" Our answer? Walk with them. Rather than put up a front that students can see through, be authentic with them. You might need to say something like this: "Hey, the more I get into this stuff, I realize how much further I have to go. But I'm motivated. I desperately want a closer walk with Jesus. So pray for me as you pray for each other. We're walking through this one together." Kids hate phonies, but love the authentic. Get real! Your students will love you for it.

4. Get Your Students Involved

The smaller the group, the more conversational you will want to make the sessions. Ask open-ended questions, the kind that require more than a "yes" or "no" answer. Remember, the students who read the book and devotionals have done a lot of meditating on the subjects during the week prior to your teaching. Make sure to give them opportunities to share what they have learned and applied.

5. Expect Opposition

According to the apostle Paul, our warfare is not against flesh and blood, but against spiritual forces of exceeding power. So don't be surprised when everything seems to fall apart. Don't get discouraged. One fighter pilot said that he never once flew over the right target without being fired at. So be encouraged! If the enemy's firing away, you must be on the right track! Just remember that the solution lies not in simply silencing the rowdy kids and fixing the feedback in the speaker system. Spiritual battles must be fought with spiritual weapons, like prayer, the Word and faith.

6. Pray, Pray, Pray

Samuel Chadwick once said, "Satan laughs at our toil, mocks at our wisdom, but trembles when we pray." Pray for your students by name. Pray that you can apply the material to your own life before teaching it to others. Pray for protection. Pray for revival. Pray for the eyes of lost students to be opened to the gospel.

No Equal to His Claims
Who Does This Guy Think He Is?

The Challenge 2000 Covenant

Introduce the Challenge 2000 Covenant by flashing it on a screen or holding it up on a poster board. Explain that by the end of this series, they will have the opportunity to join thousands of students across the nation who have signed this covenant, committing themselves to follow Jesus and communicate the gospel to every student.

The Hook

Begin the session by saying, **"Tonight, we're starting a series that could revolutionize our lives, and send you into school a different person. It's already starting to change my life, and I can't wait to see what will happen to the ones who grab this message and go with it all the way. To begin I want to read a poem inspired by the Littleton tragedy. Listen carefully."**

"The Outsider"
by Dave Tippett

He was a dweeb in the eyes of some.
A loner.
Strange.
Unpredictable.
He was different.
Spoke of strange things.
Weird things.
Things that no one had heard before.
His dad had a bad reputation with some.
He tried to talk about his relationship with his father.
Few of the teachers listened. Or cared.
He belonged to a gang.
A gang that was considered dangerous.
It roamed the town, causing local authorities trouble.
He got in people's faces.
He hung out with losers.
Rich kids hated him.
Some said Satan was in him.
He called the teachers names.
To their faces.
He lived on the streets.
He called himself God.
He got violent once. He was expelled for it. But he came back.
He talked about his own death calmly.

the main point

By the end of this session, students should become so intrigued with the person of Jesus Christ that they will choose to devote time each day to pursue Him.

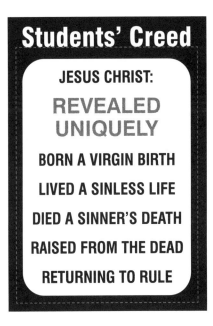

Students' Creed

JESUS CHRIST:
REVEALED UNIQUELY
BORN A VIRGIN BIRTH

LIVED A SINLESS LIFE

DIED A SINNER'S DEATH

RAISED FROM THE DEAD

RETURNING TO RULE

Preparation:
Passion: Better Is One Day CD to play as students enter and exit; *Listen: Louder* CD; CD player. Ask a student or two ahead of time to prepare a short testimony about their impressions of Jesus before they became Christians.

He promised to come back from the dead.
One of his gang got him arrested.
He defended himself in court. He lost.
The state executed him. It was a horrible death.
On the third day, he kept his promise.[1]

Comment, **"For most of us, when we first hear this poem, the last person we think it's referring to is Jesus. Maybe that's because the picture many people have in their minds of Jesus may bear little resemblance to that Man who wasn't afraid to challenge the powerful leaders of His day—the Man who made such an impact on the world that His birth split all of human history between B.C. ('Before Christ') and A.D. ('In the year of our Lord')."**

The Message

The Jesus Who Never Lived

Some students could share the impressions they had of Jesus before they became Christians. Perhaps call a student or two during the week to prepare a short testimony in this regard. They could share at this point.

Then say, **"The song I played in the background of your discussion said that there is something unique about Jesus. To understand what sets Him apart from others, let's first put some names on several popular, but warped pictures of Jesus."**

1. "Mr. Nice Guy"

Sort of a first-century Mr. Rogers, He always spoke kindly, made everyone happy and would never get upset with anyone. Each morning He would wake his disciples by singing, "It's a Beautiful Day in the Neighborhood."

2. "The Party Pooper"

He was a solemn religious figure who sought out fun-loving people so that He could tell them to shut up and get back to work.

3. "The Wimp"

He probably believed in turning the other cheek because He knew He'd get pounded if He tried to resist.

4. "The Conformist"

Jesus was a first-century preppie who related well to those always involved in church, ever concerned about what people think, having the right car, the right clothes and 2.5 smiling, well-adjusted children.

MUSIC
SUGGESTION:

Play a portion of the song "Come Like You Promise," by Delirious?, from the *Listen: Louder* CD. Ask, **"Why was (and is) there such a great expectation for Jesus' coming?"**

SMALL GROUP
DISCUSSION:

Pictures of Jesus
Many people don't want to become Christians because their picture of Jesus is messed up. Break your students into groups of four or five and have them try to describe the pictures of Jesus that non-Christians have. In other words, what do they *think* Jesus is like? After a few minutes, have someone from each group report what they discovered.

5. "Teacher of the Year"

He was not the Son of God, but just a great teacher who put things like no one had heard them before.

Will the Real Jesus *Please* Stand Up?

Comment, **"A talk-show host used to have a time on his show where he would discuss 'Things that make you go Hmmmm?' Well, I've got something that ought to make a lot of people go 'Hmmmm?' If Jesus really was that wimpy conformist or party pooper that so many people envision, then why was His coming foretold, and why would anyone in the first century have ever followed Him? Why would He have left such a mark on history that almost 2000 years after His death, tens of thousands of people would begin wearing WWJD (What Would Jesus Do?) bracelets to work and to school? Something's seriously wrong with the pictures of Jesus that most people have. Let's take a look at some Scriptures to discover the real Jesus."**

Large Group Activity

Gathering the Facts

People today have all kinds of weird ideas about Jesus. To get a better picture of the real Jesus of history, have students imagine that they are newspaper reporters, trying to write an article on this controversial figure named Jesus. What kind of people would they want to interview to get facts? *(Eyewitnesses.)* In their research, they discover that four men took the time to write accounts of His life, two of whom, John and Matthew, were actual eyewitnesses. Mark and Luke got their information from eyewitness sources.

Ask for several volunteers to read the Scriptures listed in this activity from these eyewitness accounts of Jesus, so that they can get the real picture of just who He was.

"The thief comes only to steal and kill and destroy; I have come that they may have life, and have it to the full. I am the good shepherd. The good shepherd lays down his life for the sheep" (John 10:10, 11).

"Doesn't sound like someone who's out to ruin our lives. So cross off picture number 2."

"Jesus entered the temple area and drove out all who were buying and selling there. He overturned the tables of the money changers and the benches of those selling doves. 'It is written,' he said to them, 'My house will be called a house of prayer,' but you are making it a 'den of robbers'" (Matthew 21:12, 13).

"Woe to you, teachers of the law and Pharisees, you hypocrites! You travel over land and sea to win a single convert, and when he becomes one, you make him twice as much a son of hell as you are . . . . you are like whitewashed tombs, which look beautiful on the

MUSIC SUGGESTION:

While they are discussing, play the song "There's Something About That Name," by Sonic Flood and Kevin Max from the *Listen: Louder* CD, softly in the background.

outside but on the inside are full of dead men's bones and everything unclean" (Matthew 23:15, 27).

Jesus was not afraid to challenge the leadership of His day. These are not exactly the words and actions of a politically correct, conformist wimp. So cross off pictures 1, 3 and 4.

"So, I suppose that knocks out all of the popular pictures of Jesus, except for the picture of Him as a mere human who was a star teacher. But would you consider a mere human being only a great teacher if He said the following things about Himself?"

"Jesus answered, 'I am the way and the truth and the life. No one comes to the Father except through me. If you really knew me, you would know my Father as well. From now on, you do know him and have seen him'" (John 14:6, 7).

"The only way to God? Now wait a minute! That's a pretty big claim! And it doesn't sound very tolerant!"

"When Jesus saw their faith, he said to the paralytic, 'Son, your sins are forgiven'" (Mark 2:5).

"The authority to forgive sins? You may say, 'So what? I forgive my sister all the time.' True. We forgive those who have done something against us. But we can't forgive someone who's sinned, not against us, but against God. Who does this guy think He is?"

"'I tell you the truth,' Jesus answered, 'before Abraham was born, I am!'" (John 8:58).

"Lived before Abraham? Is this guy a nut?"

"I and the Father are one" (John 10:30).

"He claimed to be one with God!"

"Jesus answered: 'Don't you know me, Philip, even after I have been among you such a long time? Anyone who has seen me has seen the Father. How can you say, 'Show us the Father'?" (John 14:9).

"He said that anyone who has seen Him has seen the Father. So, it's beginning to look like whoever Jesus is, He's more than just a great teacher or nice guy who went around doing good deeds. In fact, Dr. John Warwick Montgomery put it this way: 'The earliest records we have of the life and ministry of Jesus give the overwhelming impression that this man went around not so much *doing good* but making a decided nuisance of himself.'"[2]

Illustration

Share the following story with students:

"Think of it this way. Imagine that a new guy named J.C. enrolls in your school and you decide to show him around. He seems

nice enough, but the more you get to know him, the more you begin to wonder. One day, while you're eating lunch with him in the lunchroom, the girl with the worst reputation in the school strikes up an intense conversation with him. Nearby, students are straining their ears to listen in. Finally, J.C. looks her in the eye and says, 'Your sins are forgiven.' One eavesdropper drops his fork. Another laughs out loud. Still another picks up his tray to leave, shaking his head in disgust. You are perplexed.

"In history class, your teacher is in the middle of covering the exploits of Napoleon, when J.C. passes you a note that says, 'Before Napoleon was born, I was alive.' You keep waiting for him to turn around and laugh, but he never does.

"Finally, some jock types corner J.C. at his locker and confront him. 'Hey, just who do you think you are?' Without missing a beat, he looks at them and says, 'I and my Father God are one. If you've seen me, you've seen my Father, God.'

"At this point, people aren't going to conclude that J.C. is just Mr. Nice Guy. And if he begins to sing 'It's a Beautiful Day in the Neighborhood,' don't expect anyone to join in on the chorus. In fact, most of us would expect him to see a counselor and transfer to the place with padded walls and shrinks in white coats."

A Memorable Day at School

"But let's imagine that J.C.'s outrageous statements have a day or two to circulate around the school. As 'J.C. Jokes' start replacing 'blonde jokes,' he decides it's time to give some evidence that his claims are true.

"The bread truck misses its delivery, so at lunch J.C. takes a dinner roll from someone's lunch box and divides it to feed the entire student body. 'Can't be,' mumble some. 'Must be a magician. Yeah, like a teenage David Copperfield,' conclude others. But over the next few days you and your friends gasp in amazement as J.C. gives sight to a ninth grader everyone knew was born blind. Your school newspaper promptly assigns a reporter to stick to this guy like glue.

"After school you notice him standing by the pool one day at swim practice. With everyone's eye on him, he casually walks across the pool lengthwise to reach your team manager, who is crippled from a childhood bout with polio. All eyes are on him as he says, 'Get up!' and she begins to walk normally.

"The next day at school the halls are a beehive of conversation about this guy. Then, a hush comes over the crowd as he enters. Following him are the two seniors who died in the car accident last weekend! They claim that he raised them from the dead at the funeral home! 'Now,' says J.C., 'are you ready to consider my claims?'"

After you have shared the illustration, point out to students these

TEACHING TIP:

This is a long story to tell. Your temptation will be to simply read it to your students, or try to memorize it word for word. Resist both. Instead, read the story over a couple of times, until you can "see" the story in your mind. In that way, you can tell the story naturally, like you would relate the event if you had seen it firsthand.

If you are fearful of forgetting a major point, simply highlight three or four phrases such as, "enrolls," "girl with worst reputation," "In history class," jock types," bread truck," "standing by the pool," "he raised them from the dead." Then, in a glance, you can see where you are.

are the type of things that Jesus did to back up His claims. So, that leaves us with a choice about which picture we're going to accept about Jesus. Say, **"I love the way C. S. Lewis put it. He was a former skeptic who became a Christian while teaching at Oxford. It's kind of a long quote, but it's worth hearing:**

"'I am trying here to prevent anyone saying the really foolish thing that people often say about Him: "I'm ready to accept Jesus as a great moral teacher, but I don't accept His claim to be God." That is the one thing we must not say. A man who was merely a man and said the sort of things Jesus said would not be a great moral teacher. He would either be a lunatic, on a level with the man who says he is a poached egg, or else he would be the Devil of Hell. You must make your choice. Either this man was, and is, the Son of God: or else a madman or something worse. You can shut Him up for a fool, you can spit at Him and kill Him as a demon; or you can fall at His feet and call Him Lord and God. But let us not come with any patronising nonsense about His being a great human teacher. He has not left that open to us. He did not intend to.'"[3]

After you have read this quote, ask students:
- **Do you get what Lewis is saying here? Is he saying that Jesus wasn't a good, moral teacher?** (*No. He's saying that Jesus was a good, moral teacher. But He was much more.*)
- **Why can we not accept the picture of Jesus as being simply a human moral teacher, but not the Son of God?** (*Because a good, moral teacher who was not God would never claim to be God. His claims would show him to be a deluded egomaniac.*)

The Application

So, what do we do with this Jesus? As a result of this session, some of your students may realize that the picture of Jesus they've carried around must have been a picture of someone else. Perhaps they've come face to face with the radical claims of Jesus for the first time.

Conclude by saying, **"Some of us have already begun a six-week quest for the real Jesus, where we'll get to know more intimately the most unique person in all of human history. If you missed last week, it's not too late to get in on our quest. Here's how to get the most out of it. Read a chapter each week in the book that goes along with this series: *Jesus no equal*. Spend some one-on-one time with Jesus each day, using the *Jesus no equal* devotionals, which you will find at the end of each chapter. When something really touches your life, put a star by it so that you will remember to share it with us at our next meeting."**

You may also want to encourage students to purchase a copy of the *Passion: Better Is One Day* CD to use in their personal worship. This CD captures live the exciting worship of thousands of college students.

No Equal to His Humility
He Did What?

The Hook

Begin this session by saying, **"Some of you have probably heard this story which has circulated on the Internet. Some might debate the specific details of the story. It seems that in the mid-'80s a teenager named Brian Warner began attending a local youth group. He was sort of an awkward kid, and no one really wanted to talk to him. The youth pastor would approach him, and do the usual youth pastor thing. You know, 'How are you . . . that's good . . .' and then talk to other kids. One day the youth group went to an amusement park, and the youth pastor paired kids up for safety, but no one wanted to pair with Brian. So he walked around the park by himself. The pastor didn't think he really needed to talk to Brian about God because Brian had gone to a Christian school. Brian attended church for about 3½ months, but one day he just stopped coming.**

"A few years later, the youth pastor received a call from one of his former high school students. The young man asked his former pastor if he remembered a student named Brian Warner. After some description, he remembered him. The guy asked, 'Do you know who he is now?' The pastor said no. He gave him a hint, 'He doesn't go by Brian anymore.' The pastor was stumped. The student replied, 'Brian Warner is now known as Marilyn Manson.'"

Allow students to respond to the story. They may also talk about some of the other stories concerning Manson that have circulated. Then comment, **"Whether or not all of these details are true, in popular culture today there may be no one person who represents and promotes a rebellious, godless lifestyle more effectively than Marilyn Manson. But you have to wonder: What if some Christians in Brian Warner's youth group or school had reached out to him, invited him to some church trips, fought over getting to sit with him on the bus and hung out with him when they arrived? You have to wonder: Would there ever have been a Marilyn Manson?**

"Today we're going to look at some people who refused to swallow the social divisions of their day. Instead of clawing their way to the top of the social ladder, they were more concerned about the misfits, the ones at the bottom of the ladder, the 'Brian Warners' who are losing in your school's social game. The first one we will look at gave us the ultimate example."

As you move into the message of the day, take a few minutes to invite God's presence into your meeting. Ask God to speak through you. Ask your students to pray silently that God will speak to them.

the main point

By the end of this session, students should know how Jesus humbled Himself to reach them, and be willing to humble themselves to accept and reach others.

Students' Creed

JESUS CHRIST:

REVEALED UNIQUELY

BORN A VIRGIN BIRTH

LIVED A SINLESS LIFE

DIED A SINNER'S DEATH

RAISED FROM THE DEAD

RETURNING TO RULE

Preparation:
Passion: Better Is One Day CD to play as students enter and exit; *Listen: Louder* CD; CD player; note cards and pencils; copies of "The Snoot Exam" for each student; PowerPoint®, a transparency and an overhead projector or chalkboard and chalk.

PowerPoint is a registered trademark of Microsoft Corporation in the United States and/or other countries.

VIDEO SUGGESTION:

Show a 30-second clip of a Marilyn Manson video that would be appropriate to use in your setting. Be careful not to play too much! Then ask, **"Does anyone know who is singing? What do you know about his life?"**

The Message

From Heaven to Earth

Have one or several of the students read Philippians 2:5-8 aloud. You may want to share this passage by reading it from *The Message*:

"Think of yourselves the way Christ Jesus thought of himself. He had equal status with God but didn't think so much of himself that he had to cling to the advantages of that status no matter what. Not at all. When the time came, he set aside the privileges of deity and took on the status of a slave, became human! Having become human, he stayed human. It was an incredibly humbling process. He didn't claim special privileges. Instead, he lived a selfless, obedient life and then died a selfless, obedient death—and the worst kind of death at that: a crucifixion."

After the Scripture has been read, have students interact with the following questions. (Ahead of time, you will want to put these questions in a PowerPoint® presentation, or write them on a transparency or on the chalkboard.)

Say, **"These questions should help us see what kind of social fall Jesus took. Talk about them for a few minutes in your small groups. Then, I'll let a few of you report to the entire group."**

- **What was life like for Jesus before He came to earth?**
- **How do you think He was treated by the angels in Heaven?**
- **According to the passage, in what ways did He humble Himself?** *(He made Himself nothing, took on the nature of a servant, appearance of a man, death on a cross.)*
- **What's especially humbling about death by crucifixion?** *(You can't take care of your bodily needs, stripped of clothes, taunted and despised as a criminal.)*
- **What does this passage say to those who feel insignificant?** *(If God did all this for you, you must be worth something. No matter where you see yourself on the social ladder, you have incredible worth. Since God made you and Jesus died for you, never put yourself down.)*

Large Group Activity

After the students' discussion, invite them to come back to the large group. Say, **"The 'so what?' of this passage of Scripture is pretty obvious, but in case the 'demon of duh' just flew over a few heads, we'll let the apostle Paul spell it out for us. Who will read verses 3-5 for us?"**

After one of the students has done so, discuss these questions:

- **What do these verses say to those who look down on others?** *(If Jesus humbled Himself to come for you, then you should humble yourself to serve others. The bottom line is this: Don't ever call someone a nerd for whom Christ died.)*
- **What social divisions exist in your school?**
- **Are these groups just convenient ways for similar people to**

SMALL GROUP
DISCUSSION:

Divide into groups of four or five and ask students to turn in their Bibles to Philippians 2:5-8, to read about the greatest social fall of all time. Appoint someone to read the passage aloud. As it is read, think about how this passage challenges the cliques in schools.

VIDEO
SUGGESTION:

Show three short clips from the movie *Back to the Future, Part I*. The first clip is the family scene where the father is a nerd. The second clip shows Marty in the past where he encourages his father about his science fiction writing. The final clip goes back to the future, where Marty's father brings in his published book. Use these clips to point out how one who is not expected to be anything can rise to fame.

get together, or do the groups exclude and hurt people?

"To contrast Jesus' attitude with most of our attitudes, let me set up one more discussion: Imagine that you get off the school bus one day and find an old bottle on the side of the road. As you wipe off the dirt and grime to get a closer look, a strange mist fills the air and you find yourself before a huge genie who says his term is about to expire, but he has one wish left to grant. He says, 'Tomorrow, you can go to school a new person. I can transform you into whatever person you want to be. Just choose the look you want, IQ, personality, bank account and social status.'

"Did it ever occur to you that Jesus had the power to choose whatever form He wanted to take when He came to earth? But instead of coming as a *dominant* Roman, He entered the world as one of the *dominated* Jews. Instead of entering a rich family, He came into a poor one, and had to work for a living as a carpenter. Instead of hanging out with the social elite, He wasn't ashamed to befriend fishermen and despised tax gatherers.

"So, what's the point? Let's go back to the genie situation. You're just about to ask the genie to morph you into this ideal person, when you happen to notice your 'WWJD' bracelet. So you ask yourself, 'What would Jesus do?' What would Jesus tell the genie?"

Ask students for their response to this question.

Continue by saying, "Some of you might say, 'I'd still want to be that ideal person, but for a good reason. You see, if I could make it to the top of the ladder, I could be more effective in leading others to Christ.' But you know what? Jesus could put you up there in an instant if He thought that was the most effective way for you to minister. If you're there, use that platform, but seeing how Jesus decided to come down, I wonder if He's got some incredible plans for the rest of us—right where we are."

The Great Reverse

Continue this imaginary scenario by asking, "What if, instead of clawing our way up the social ladder like everyone else, we turned around and started paying attention to those who are where we are, and especially those below us on the social ladder? No matter how much of a geek you think you are in other people's eyes, has it ever occurred to you that kids a couple of years younger than you might think it's cool to hang out with you? Have you ever thought of the impact you could have on a little brother or sister if you swallowed your pride and took some interest in him or her?

"Jesus is urging us to do something totally counterculture. While everyone else floats downstream, He's asking us to turn around and swim upstream."

Optional Idea

Construct the Ideal You! Allow students to take up the genie's challenge, lay aside any superspiritual thoughts and sculpt the ultimate guy or girl that they would like to become. Have some fun with this! Write characteristics of the ultimate girl on one side of a blackboard or overhead, the ultimate guy on the other side. They may say things like "the IQ of Einstein," "the bank account of Bill Gates," the looks of a favorite movie star, "the athletic talent of Michael Jordan," etc.).

Share the following with students:

"Just try inviting Steven Spielberg or George Lucas to your next party. Now that they're famous, there's no way they're coming. But if you had been their classmates in school and had invited them over, they might have come. You know why? Because they weren't getting much attention back then.

Spielberg didn't dress right in middle school. And he wasn't good at sports. Lucas was a little shrimp who made 'Ds' and was considered a loser. Neither were popular. They wouldn't have gotten you anywhere by sitting with them at lunch. And some of you might have snooted them. Just think, those students that your classmates have labeled 'geeks' and 'dweebs' may be tomorrow's Lucases and Spielbergs!"

Spend some time letting students respond to these questions:

- How can helping the lowly help our friendships?
- What do most people think of snoots?
- What do you think when you see someone get "snooted"?

Comment, "How many students have you ever heard say, 'You know why I love that guy so much? Because he can't stand people who aren't his social equal.' In contrast, those who accept others get more real friends."

The Snoot Exam

Ahead of time, you will need to make enough photocopies of "The Snoot Exam" on the next page. Distribute the exam and writing utensils to students. Give them sufficient time to read the instructions, then take the test. After they have done so, bring them back together and say, **"So, we can see how far short most of us fall. But why is it so hard to live out this teaching? Why is it so tough to reach down the ladder instead of up?"**

Get responses from students. Some possible answers include: *We risk our social status because everyone else looks down on those people; we're terrified that people will think we're a part of their social group; we're afraid that if we accept them, they'll hang to us like glue, and try to hang around when we're with our other friends.*

Is It Worth the Risk?

Say, **"In order to better answer this question, let's read what happened to Jesus after His dramatic dive to the bottom of the social ladder."** Read Philippians 2:9-11 aloud. Then ask:

- **How did Jesus' journey down the ladder pay off in the end?**
- **Was it worth it?**

(Sure, He was pretty lowly for 33 years on earth. But for the past 2000 years, He's been honored in Heaven. And Jesus says that we will go through the same process. Look at Luke 14:11; 18:14; and Matthew 5:5. We have to humble ourselves to be exalted, make ourselves poor to become rich, die to ourselves to get a life. Each of us needs to decide whether we're going to seek our glory for a little while here, or Christ's glory forever in Heaven.)

- **Do you get a good feeling when you've helped somebody?**
- **How did Jesus' journey down the ladder help others?**

(Now we have a way to Heaven. So, our second reason to go against the flow is because we care for people. And often it's easier to minister to people while they are at the bottom of the ladder.)

The Awesome Power of Acceptance

"We introduced this session with the awesome power of 'snooting,' and how it helped create Marilyn Manson. Let's conclude with the awesome power of acceptance, and how it transformed a high school freshman we'll call 'Ted.'

"Ted was one of those awkward, nerdy types who wasn't good at sports and whose words seldom came out quite right. To make matters worse, he was rather outgoing. But some upperclassmen took an interest in Ted, inviting him to go to weekday Bible studies and backing up their sincerity by offering him a weekly ride. Through these guys, Jesus began working in Ted's life.

"Athletics wasn't Ted's thing. When he attended summer camp, he wasn't an asset to his volleyball team. So, to keep their team from losing, a jock or two remedied the situation by drawing a

The Snoot Exam

Let's take an imaginary trip to the doctor, not for a physical exam, but a pride exam. No one else will see your responses, so answer honestly. In case you don't know what a "snoot" is, could a few students volunteer to line up across the front, facing the group, and give us some expressions that the fashion and social police use? When you try to talk to someone who thinks she is cooler than you, and she turns up her nose or makes it obvious that she doesn't want to be seen around you, you have been snooted.

So, are you a snoot? Here's the test. Remember, it's just for you, so be honest. Circle the correct number in each instance.

1 = Never   **2 = Seldom**   **3 = Sometimes**   **4 = Often**   **5 = Always**

1. Are there certain cars you would not be caught dead in?
   1   2   3   4   5

2. Do people have to dress in a certain way to be in your group?
   1   2   3   4   5

3. Do you make jokes about people who aren't as smart, or aren't as sharp as you?
   1   2   3   4   5

4. Do you make jokes about people who don't have as much as you?
   1   2   3   4   5

5. Do you use words like geek, dweeb, etc. to refer to others?
   1   2   3   4   5

6. Do you avoid certain people because of the color of their skin?
   1   2   3   4   5

7. If you're with a certain group, and an acquaintance who doesn't fit with that group walks up, do you ever ignore or brush off that person?
   1   2   3   4   5

Now, tally up your score. Here's how the results look:
Score:
30-35   You're a major snoot!
15-29   You need to swallow your pride.
8-14   You still need a little work.
7   You should be teaching this lesson!

Play "Humble Thyself" from the *Listen: Louder* CD as students complete their cards. They could join in singing it at the end.

ILLUSTRATION: _____

People respected Albert Einstein because of his genius, but they loved him because of his total disregard of people's social status. One day, a nine-year-old girl came to his house, needing some help with her math homework. Gladly, he let her in and helped her each day over a period of time with her work. Now think about it. Here was a man who was considered the most brilliant man of his time, who had piles of mail from "important" people that he didn't have time to answer, and invitations to go anywhere and do almost anything he wanted. But he often preferred the company of the "little" people of the world, and people loved him for it.

MUSIC
SUGGESTION: _____

A great way to close this session would be by playing the song "A Little More," by Jennifer Knapp on the *Listen: Louder* CD. It emphasizes the grace of God that comes to us in Jesus. Point out the lyric, "For all the sin that lives in me, it took a nail to set me free." Spend some time thanking Jesus for humbling Himself and coming down to show us how to live. Understanding how He laid down His life for us motivates us to be gracious toward all groups of people.

circle around Ted in the dirt and instructing him to stay there. They would hit the balls that came near him.

"After the game, someone felt sorry for Ted and said, 'Hey, I feel bad about some folks putting you down back there. I just wanted to tell you that I really admire your walk with God.' The encourager would never forget Ted's response. He said, 'You know, I think the reason I love God so much is that I just can't do anything else.'"

Bring the story home to students by asking the poignant question:

• Isn't it strange how often the ones we meet who seem to have the least potential, may have the most potential in God's eyes?

Conclude, **"Ted went on to study law at a prestigious university. While he was there, he continued to love God, and became a student leader in a Christian organization, sharing the gospel especially with incoming freshmen. Today, he's a faithful Christian leader."**

The Application

What are your students going to do with all this? Jesus demonstrated the ultimate example of humility when He came way down the social ladder to rescue them. Are they willing to do the same for others?

Challenge them with these words: **"Let's think about our own schools, neighborhoods and homes. Do you know some outsiders like 'Ted,' misfits like Brian Warner, loners like Spielberg and losers like Lucas?"**

Distribute note cards and pencils to students. Ask them to draw a large ladder on the card, and on each rung put the initials of one or more people that they believe God wants them to "reach down to" this week.

After they have done that, comment, **"Now, look down at those initials. They represent people with hurts, fears and dreams—just like you. But nobody seems to care what's going on inside of them. Will you care? An excellent way to start might be to simply look them in the eye, ask 'How are you doing today?' and really mean it."**

As you close, remind students, **"Read chapter three this week in the book *Jesus no equal*. Spend some one-on-one time with Jesus each day, using the *Jesus no equal* devotionals, which you will find at the end of the chapter. When something grabs you, put a star by it so that you will remember to share it with us at our next meeting."**

No Equal to His Servanthood
You Want Me to Love *Them*?

The Hook

To begin your session, play a game called "Invasion of the Body Snatchers." This can be played in a medium-sized room or a marked-off area outside. Choose two fast students to be the "aliens" who hold hands and "snatch" (touch) others. Once snatched, the person who is touched becomes an alien, and must join hands with the other extraterrestrials. Once four aliens are together, they can divide into groups of two, and so on until all students in your group have been snatched.

After you have played the game, comment, **"Imagine that you're an alien, sent to Earth to start an invasion of the body snatchers. The only problem is that your boss has put you on a tight schedule. He wants all of America's students within three months. So, there's no time to go slowly from person to person. Somehow, you've got to draw crowds of students, and have the ability to touch thousands in a day. Your solution? Start by snatching youth culture heroes, so they can do a publicity tour of America's major cities.**

"To find those heroes, you sneak into some students' bedrooms, looking for posters on their walls that reveal their heroes. From looking at the posters, who would you determine are students' primary heroes?"

Allow time for students to respond. As they do, record their suggestions on an overhead transparency or a chalkboard.

Continue by saying, **"Sometimes people put up posters in their bedroom just because they like the posters. But for others, their bedroom is a shrine for their real heroes, celebrities they admire and want to be like. Do you think students are really impacted by the heroes they choose? In what way?"**

Point out that the two gunmen who pulled the trigger at Columbine High School in Littleton, Colorado, idolized Adolf Hitler. Did that say something about them?

Ask students:

• **Do you think Hitler's ideas had any impact on their values?**

• **If someone not only likes Marilyn Manson's music, but idolizes him, what kinds of things will that person likely value?**

Introduce today's topic by saying, **"Today we want to talk about the Ultimate Action Hero, why He has become my hero and why I believe He deserves to be yours."**

Ask God to speak to your students during this session.

the main point

By the end of this session, students should be motivated to follow Jesus' example of servanthood by volunteering for specific service opportunities.

Students' Creed

JESUS CHRIST:

REVEALED UNIQUELY

BORN A VIRGIN BIRTH

LIVED A SINLESS LIFE

DIED A SINNER'S DEATH

RAISED FROM THE DEAD

RETURNING TO RULE

Preparation:
Bibles; *Passion: Better Is One Day* CD to play as students enter and exit; *Listen: Louder* CD; CD player. At least a week ahead of time, look over the application section to determine how your students will serve. At the end of the message, they will participate in a service project.

The Message

Comment, **"Since our heroes influence us, it's important to choose the right ones. In your opinion, what ingredients does it take to make good heroes?"**

Let students share some of their ideas.

- **Is it merely coolness and talent, or does their character make any difference as to how you feel about them?**
- **What aspects of their character matter? Why?**

What Makes a Hero?

Present the following scenario to students:

"Imagine that one day you walk into a restaurant and see your hero, a professional baseball player, sitting at a table with some other big shots. All your life you've wanted to be like him, dreamed of meeting him, rehearsed in your mind what you would say to him if the opportunity ever came and dreamed of getting his autograph. As he and his friends get up to leave the table, you grab your napkin and a pen, walk up to him and begin to introduce yourself as an aspiring pro and his greatest fan. But before you get out half of your first sentence, he looks down at you with a smirk and says, 'You shrimp. You'll never make it in the big leagues.' Then he laughs and turns back to his friends. Do you think your opinion of him would change? How? Why?"

Allow students to respond to this situation. Then make sure they get the point that we can admire many people solely for their skill. But to be considered in the hero category, we want to know something of their character and how they treat other people.

The Ultimate Action Hero

Lead students to see why Jesus Christ has become the greatest hero of all time.

Comment, **"A major part of His popularity is because of who He is and the incredible miracles He performed. We saw that two weeks ago, when we looked at how His awesome miracles set Him apart from everyone in history. Those spectacular wonders make people _respect_ Him. But what makes people _love_ Him, and take Him as their hero?"**

To get some answers, you'll need several volunteers to look up the following five passages and read them for the group: Matthew 9:36; Luke 4:18, 19; Luke 19:10; Matthew 20:28; John 10:10.

After reading Matthew 9:36, ask:

- **How did Jesus feel about people?**

Allow time for students to respond. Then say, **"I wonder if all kinds of people were in the crowd that day. You know—some talented, some not; some who acted super cool and some first-century dweebs; some rich, some poor. But Jesus looked right through all the artificial stuff and saw their needs."**

Share this illustration with students:

"**Students at a high school were shocked when a popular athlete committed suicide. As a result, a reporter interviewed his best friend. 'You were his best friend. Do you have any idea why he took his own life?' The friend responded, 'No. I guess we were just too macho to talk about stuff like that.'**"

Continue by saying, "**How tragic! You've got to wonder if things would have been different if someone could have seen through his cool image and sensed that this guy may have gone home each Friday night to a father who berated him for every mistake he made in the game. Here's a guy who was cool on the outside, but maybe buried his head in his pillow each night and cried in despair because he couldn't meet the unrealistic expectations of his parents or coaches.**"

You may want to talk about how easy it is to walk down the hall at school, see people's outward appearances and think we've got them pegged. We swallow the stereotypes: the arrogant jocks, stuck-up preppies, freak losers, dumb rednecks. And then there are the blonde jokes! It's hard to admit it, but when we throw everybody into categories, we're prejudiced.

Continue by saying, "**But my Hero doesn't look at your student body and see cheerleaders, jocks, freaks, preppies or whatever categories you have. He has compassion for them all. That's how Jesus feels about people. Now let's discover how He treated people.**"

After a student reads Luke 4:18, 19, ask:
- **What are the four types of people Jesus came to help?** *(the poor, prisoners, blind, oppressed)*

Have someone read Luke 19:10, then say, "**If a purpose statement were written about most of us, it might read something like this, 'He or she came to seek and impress girls (or guys)' or, 'He (or she) came to seek popularity.' In case you haven't noticed, you don't have to wait in line to visit a nursing home or mow an invalid's yard. But give an opportunity to become famous and everyone shows up.**"

After Matthew 20:28 has been read, say, "**Jesus could have come down to have fun. Just imagine, He could have set up a 'Six Flags Over Jerusalem' amusement park. He could have eaten the best foods, worn the best clothes and enjoyed fame as a miracle worker. But instead of being served, He served others. He could have clicked His fingers and made the Pharisees' noses grow about a foot every time they got proud. Instead, He came to serve.**"

Finally, have a student read John 10:10, then ask, "**Are we seeing the pattern in these verses? None of the things Jesus did were wrapped around serving Himself. He came to give life to others, to serve others, to save others. And it didn't matter whether they were big time or small potatoes. While some snubbed the children, He**

ILLUSTRATION: _____

By the end of 1996, parents had taken 3,600 children to read for the roles of Anakin Skywalker and the young Queen Amidala in the new *Star Wars* trilogy.[1] Contrast their search for fame with what Jesus came to do.

welcomed them. And He shocked people by talking to a prostitute and treating her like a real person. Instead of pushing around His disciples, He washed their feet. And, of course, in the end He performed the ultimate act of servanthood by dying in our place."

Challenge students to contrast the heroes that decorate so many bedroom walls with the life and character of Jesus. Ask, "**What did those people ever do for you? Some heroes care nothing about other people. They are totally obsessed with themselves. But, Jesus is always there, caring for you as someone who has great worth in His eyes, enough for Him to die for you.**"

Choose Your Hero

Say something like this: "**Successful people choose their heroes carefully. They choose people they want to be like. For instance, actor Michael J. Fox put up pictures of famous comedians in his house. Albert Einstein hung a picture in his office of Isaac Newton, one of the greatest scientists of all time.**

"**What kind of pictures do you think Arnold Schwarzenegger had in his bedroom as a teenager? As you listen to Arnold's story, think what the world would be like if only we could follow our spiritual hero with the same intensity that Schwarzenegger followed his bodybuilding hero.**"

Then, tell the following story:

"**At 15 years old, Arnold Schwarzenegger decided he wanted to be the best bodybuilder in the world. And when he saw a massive bodybuilder named Reg Park in a movie, he knew he had found his hero. In Schwarzenegger's own words, 'From that point on I was utterly dominated by Reg Park. His image was my ideal. I found out everything I could about Reg Park. I bought all the magazines that published his programs. I learned how he started training, what he ate, how he lived, and how he did his workouts. I became obsessed with Reg Park; he was the image in front of me from the time I started training. . . . I pasted his pictures on all the walls of my bedroom. . . . I studied every photograph of him I could get my hands on—noting the size of his chest, arms, thighs, back and abdominals. This inspired me to work even harder. When I felt my lungs burning as though they would burst and my veins bulging with blood, I loved it. I knew then that I was growing, making one more step toward becoming like Reg Park.'**"[2]

Lead students to imagine what it would be like if Christians followed Jesus as passionately as Schwarzenegger followed Reg Park. Ask students these piercing questions:

- **What if this world were to see a new generation of Christians—who were more than church members, more than Bible-study attenders, more than nice people, but passionate followers of Christ?**
- **What if a group of students became obsessed with Jesus—**

MUSIC
SUGGESTION:

Play the song "Your Faithfulness," by Chasing Furies, from the *Listen: Louder* CD. Listen as the group sings about what Jesus has done for them. As students listen, ask them to write down the things about Jesus that the singer admires. Ask, "**What do you think the singer means when she sings, 'But the road You walk, it breaks my heart'?**"

longing to hang around the people that Jesus hung around, get in trouble with the kind of people Jesus got in trouble with, ignore popular opinion like Jesus ignored it?

- What would happen if we decided to begin serving people like Jesus served them, teaching people like Jesus taught them and having compassion on people the way Jesus had compassion on them?

Comment, **"If we could catch that vision, we could change the world. But how can we be like Jesus to the people around us?"**

Optional Activity

Bring a blindfolded student into the room three different times. The first time, everyone should yell instructions to him at the same time, while one says, at a volume no louder than the others, "Go to the table and pick up the Bible." Of course, he is confused and doesn't have a clue as to what to do.

The second time he comes in, two people should stand about the same distance from the subject, yelling out different instructions. Again, even if he understands and chooses the right directions, he is confused.

The last time, two people should give instructions again, but this time, one of them will put his arm around the subject, tell him what to do and lead him where he should go. He will follow the closest one to him.

The point is this: From the time today's students get up in the morning, they are bombarded with a ton of conflicting messages—coming at them from parents, television, music, friends, the Internet and magazines. But the one they are most likely to follow is the voice of a friend who dares to come close.

The Application

Choose one or more of the following options for maximum impact of this session on your students:

Option 1

Have a foot-washing service patterned after Jesus' example in John 13:1-17.

Option 2

Read James 1:27 and talk about the importance of "looking after orphans and widows." Then have students sign up to visit either a local nursing home, or do yard work, clean windows and gutters or whatever else is needed by some elderly members connected with your church.

Option 3

Have students bring nonperishable food items to a designated spot.

Challenge students to sacrifice something in order to buy the food, rather than just raiding their families' cupboards. Gather the groceries in several bags, and enclose a note in each bag that simply says, "In the name of Jesus." After reading Matthew 25:35, have students get in small groups to go out and deliver the food secretly. Challenge them to make their food drops on the porch, then slip away without being discovered.

Option 4

Hand out cards and envelopes so that students can write a note of encouragement to a distant relative, sick friend or someone else who might be lonely.

Option 5

Have students individually write down some service ideas they could carry out at school or at home. Encourage them to ask their parents when they get home, "What could I do to help more around the home, or with a younger brother or sister?"

No Equal to His Sacrifice
You Want Me to Die?

At least a week prior to this session, ask a student to prepare to give a five-minute personal testimony for your group. If the student has never been trained to do this, you will need to assist him or her in preparing one that is clear, but brief and effective. Ahead of time, place a decision card and pencil under each seat.

During this session, students will have the opportunity to accept the gift of salvation through Jesus. If your church or group uses a particular tract or method of evangelism, you may choose to use it during that particular part of this session. If you use a tract or booklet, consider giving each student more than one so that he can share his faith with a friend after today's session.

If some of your students are trained in sharing the gospel, talk to them a week ahead of time about this, then let them share the gospel in small groups.

The Challenge 2000 Covenant

Remind students of the Challenge 2000 Covenant by including it in your PowerPoint® presentation, flashing it on an overhead or holding it up on a poster board. Explain that in two weeks they will have the opportunity to join thousands of students across the nation who have signed this covenant, committing themselves to follow Jesus and communicate the gospel to every student in this country.

The Hook

Begin this session by asking the following question: **"What do the following people have in common?**

"You would have thought this professional football player had it made. He was a superstar who had set a record for rushing. But one day, a magazine interviewer asked him what he feared. An interesting question for a player so quick and powerful that his opponents feared him. His answer was revealing. What did he fear? In his own words, 'Dying and going to hell. But I hope I don't, because I've been a good person.'

"Chris Farley, the successful comedian who starred in 'Saturday Night Live' and many movies, including *Tommy Boy*, *Beverly Hills Ninja* and *It's a Dog's Life* died at 33 years old in 1997. Farley once admitted, 'Lust, gluttony, booze and drugs are most of the things I confess to. I can't help it. I hope to God that God will forgive me my sins. I don't know.'[1]

"In a private conversation, a confident and cool high school student was asked if he gave any thought to spiritual things. He answered, 'You know, I often stay up nights just wondering if I'm

the
main point

By the end of this session, students should understand what Jesus did on the cross, then go beyond recognizing Him as their personal hero to accepting Him as their personal Savior.

Students' Creed

JESUS CHRIST:

REVEALED UNIQUELY

BORN A VIRGIN BIRTH

LIVED A SINLESS LIFE

DIED A SINNER'S DEATH

RAISED FROM THE DEAD

RETURNING TO RULE

Preparation:
Bibles; *Passion: Better Is One Day* CD to play as students enter and exit; *Listen: Louder* CD; CD player; PowerPoint®, a transparency and an overhead projector or chalkboard and chalk; preparations for the Lord's Supper, or nails; enough copies of decision cards for each student; writing utensils

Play the song "Never Gonna Let You Go," by the group Raze, which is found on the *Listen: Louder* CD. Ask students to listen for lyrics that express their own assurance of salvation, in contrast to the opening examples of those who weren't sure about their eternal home. Note especially the lyrics, "I know You're never gonna leave me" and "You'll never let me down."

VIDEO
SUGGESTION:

Play Michael W. Smith's "Secret Ambition" video which presents a very graphic depiction of Jesus on the cross. Or, you could play a clip of Jesus' crucifixion from the *Jesus* movie or *Jesus of Nazareth*.

going to heaven when I die.'"

After you have shared the quotes from these three people, ask:
- **So, what do these people have in common?** *(All of them were unsure about where they will spend eternity.)*

Share with students that these people simply were willing to voice out loud a concern that most of us keep to ourselves. Is there a way to know for certain where we will spend eternity? Today, we'll try to get some answers.

After sharing this introduction, invite God's presence into your room, asking Him to reveal Himself to your students in a powerful way.

The Message

Comment, **"We're in the middle of a series that we call *Jesus no equal*, where we've been discovering just how awesome Jesus Christ really is. Three weeks ago we saw how His awesome miracles proved He was more than just a man. The next week we saw the incredible humility Jesus showed by coming down from Heaven to appear as a lowly human, willing to hang around any social class. Last week we were awed by His servant's heart. But in order to see how Jesus can answer the deepest questions of our hearts, we've got to get a grip on what Jesus did for us on the cross."**

The Cross: What Jesus Went Through

Say, **"As I read to you Matthew's account of Jesus' final hours, remember that this is the Son of God who is going through all this for you and me. As I read, stop me every time I come to a new type of suffering Jesus endured, and tell me what it is."**

Ask for a volunteer to write each kind of suffering on the overhead or chalkboard as students call them out.

Read Matthew 27:24-50. The types of suffering include these:
- *flogged (v. 26)*
- *stripped (v. 28)*
- *wore a crown of thorns (v. 29)*
- *mocked (v. 29)*
- *spit on (v. 30)*
- *struck repeatedly on the head (v. 30)*
- *crucified (v. 35)*
- *insults hurled at Him (v. 39)*
- *insults heaped upon Him (v. 44)*
- *forsaken by His Father (v. 46)*

Large Group Discussion

Ask students, **"Do any of you remember any other details of Jesus' sufferings that were brought out in the book or devotions that you read this past week?"**

Let students share what comes to their minds. You can jog their memories with a couple of the following:

- the agony of Gethsemane
- the Roman historian Cicero called crucifixion "the most horrible torture ever devised by man"
- a description of crucifixion including suffocation
- a description of flogging with a "cat of nine tails" (nine strips of leather with lead in the end)

Comment, **"When we understand the extent of Jesus' suffering on the cross, we are again struck with just how much Jesus loved us, and how much He deserves to be our hero. But we'll miss the whole point if we don't take a step further and clear up the big questions that the guys in our introduction couldn't answer."**

- **How can I understand what Jesus did for me?**
- **How can I have a relationship with Him?**
- **How can I know whether or not I'm going to Heaven when I die?**

The Cross: What It Means to You

Continue by saying, **"The answer to these questions comes from our understanding of the cross. Jesus was doing more than telling us how much He loved us. He was doing more than giving us an inspiring example to follow."**

Recruit several students to read some verses that describe what the cross was all about. Or, you may decide to read these verses as printed from *The Message*. After each passage is read, ask someone to share in his or her own words what Jesus' death accomplished.

• **Read Romans 5:6-10**

"Christ arrives right on time to make this happen. He didn't, and doesn't, wait for us to get ready. He presented himself for this sacrificial death when we were far too weak and rebellious to do anything to get ourselves ready. And even if we hadn't been so weak, we wouldn't have known what to do anyway. We can understand someone dying for a person worth dying for, and we can understand how someone good and noble could inspire us to selfless sacrifice. But God put his love on the line for us by offering his Son in sacrificial death while we were of no use whatever to him.

"Now that we are set right with God by means of this sacrificial death, the consummate blood sacrifice, there is no longer a question of being at odds with God in any way. If, when we were at our worst, we were put on friendly terms with God by the sacrificial death of his Son, now that we're at our best, just think of how our lives will expand and deepen by means of his resurrection life!"

—*The Message*

(He died as a sacrifice for us, when we were rebellious and unable to help ourselves. Now we are no longer at odds with God.)

• **Read 2 Corinthians 5:20, 21**

"We're Christ's representatives. God uses us to persuade men and women to drop their differences and enter into God's work of making things right between them. We're speaking for Christ himself now:

Play the song "It Is Well," which has been covered by Audio Adrenaline on the *Listen: Louder* CD. Before playing it, say, **"A successful Chicago lawyer wrote a song about the peace and assurance that comes from trusting in Jesus' finished work on the cross. His wife and four daughters were on a ship to Europe when they struck another ship. It sank in only twelve minutes, taking the lives of his daughters. He took a ship out to meet his wife, and when they neared the spot where the tragedy had occurred, he wrote this famous hymn.[2] Listen to the assurance this man found to help him through this tragedy."**

Become friends with God; he's already a friend with you. How? you say. In Christ. God put on him the wrong who never did anything wrong, so we could be put right with God."

—The Message

(He became sin on the cross for us, so that we could be considered righteous before God.)

• **Read 1 Peter 3:18**

"That's what Christ did definitively: suffered because of others' sins, the Righteous One for the unrighteous ones. He went through it all—was put to death and then made alive—to bring us to God."

—The Message

(He died for our sins and put us back into a relationship with God.)

After students have looked at these passages of Scripture, comment, **"Jesus didn't just come to earth to be our example. He came to die on the cross for us, so that we could be brought back into a right relationship with God and have eternal life with Him. To put it another way: If our biggest problem were a lack of friends, God would have sent us a companion. If our biggest problem were a lack of education, God would have sent us a tutor. But since our biggest problem is that we are lost, God sent us a Savior."**

The Cross: Making It Personal

At this point, have a student share a clear testimony of how he or she accepted the gift of eternal life through Jesus.

Afterward, thank the student, then say, **"There are three kinds of people here today: Some of you are confused, others are lost, still others are hungry. What do I mean?**

"Some of you have prayed a prayer for salvation in the past, perhaps at a camp or at a church, but today you aren't sure if you completely understood it or truly meant it. Today you have the opportunity to clear up those doubts.

"Some of you have never accepted Jesus into your life. Perhaps you've admired Jesus, but have never taken the step to make Him your personal Lord and Savior. Today you'll have the opportunity to make that decision.

"Finally, some of you have understood the gospel, accepted Christ into your life and know for certain that you have eternal life. But you want more. You are hungry to let go of more of your life, have more of Jesus and give Him away to your friends.

"So for everyone here, there is nothing more important than understanding and acting on the following four facts. Listen carefully."

Fact #1: God Loves Us and Created Us to Know Him.

• **God loves us.**

Jesus said, *"For God so loved the world that he gave his one and only Son, that whoever believes in him shall not perish but have eternal life"* (John 3:16).

- **God created us.**

  We read in the Bible, *"For you [God] created my inmost being; you knit me together in my mother's womb"* (Psalm 139:13).
- **God wants us to know Him.**

  God's Word tells us, *"Now this is eternal life: that they may know you, the only true God, and Jesus Christ, whom you have sent"* (John 17:3).

  Since fact #1 is true, why is it that many people don't know God?

Fact #2: Our Sins Keep Us from Knowing God.

Some people think of sin as getting drunk or telling lies. True, but sin involves much more.

- **What is sin?**

  We choose to disobey God and go our own way. *"We all, like sheep, have gone astray, each of us has turned to his own way"* (Isaiah 53:6).
- **Who has sinned?**

  Everyone. In the Bible we read, *"For all have sinned and fall short of the glory of God"* (Romans 3:23).
- **What happens when we sin?**

  Sin results in separation from God, leading to death and judgment. *"For the wages of sin is death"* (Romans 6:23), and, *"Just as man is destined to die once, and after that to face judgment"* (Hebrews 9:27).

  As long as sin separates us from God, we cannot know Him.
  What, then, is the solution to our separation from God?

Fact #3: We Can Know God Only Through Jesus Christ.

- **Jesus died for our sin.**

  The Bible says, *"But God demonstrates his own love for us in this: While we were still sinners, Christ died for us"* (Romans 5:8).
- **Jesus rose from the dead to give us life.**

  "We were therefore buried with him through baptism into death in order that, just as Christ was raised from the dead through the glory of the Father, we too may live a new life" (Romans 6:4).
- **Jesus opened the way for us to know God.**

  "For Christ died for sins once for all, the righteous for the unright-eous, to bring you to God" (1 Peter 3:18).

  The life, death and resurrection of Jesus Christ bridged the gap from God to us. How can we know Jesus Christ personally?

Fact #4: To Know God We Must Receive Jesus Christ.

Many people know *about* God, but don't know Him *personally*. The only way to know God personally is to receive Jesus Christ. So how can we receive Him?

- **Turn away from our sin.**

  Jesus said, *"The time has come. . . . Repent and believe the good news!"* (Mark 1:15). To repent means to *turn away* from sin.
- **Believe in Jesus.**

  "Believe in the Lord Jesus, and you will be saved" (Acts 16:31). To

believe means to *turn to* Jesus.

Jesus promises, *"Here I am! I stand at the door and knock. If anyone hears my voice and opens the door, I will come in and eat with him, and he with me"* (Revelation 3:20).

Is there any reason why you cannot choose Jesus Christ as your Lord and Savior?

The Application

Ask students, **"What did you understand about the cross that you haven't understood before?"**

Allow time for them to respond.

Continue by saying, **"Everyone here has the opportunity to make a significant decision about Jesus—to embrace the cross. One of the following categories represents you."**

- **You have been confused—you feel like you have been a follower of Jesus, but you aren't sure if it was just facts in your head or knowing for sure Jesus lives in your heart.**
- **You have been lost—you realize you have never opened your life to Jesus. You need to turn away from your sin and ask Jesus into your life. Instead of being lost, you will be found by Jesus.**
- **You have been hungry—ask Jesus to make you even more passionate about Him. Ask Him to give you a greater desire to live for and tell others about Him.**

As you close this session, you will want to lead in prayer or challenge students to further study with you or another spiritual leader in your group or church concerning what it means to be a Christian.

The Cross: Embracing It Daily

Invite students to look under their seats and find the decision card. There should be a place to mark the decision they have each made, depending on where they are in their discovery of Jesus. Tell them that as a result of their filling out the card, you will be able to better pray for them in their walk with Christ.

Conclude by saying, **"I hope you made one of these significant decisions. Whatever decision you made, Jesus wants you to follow Him passionately. Once we understand what Jesus did for us on the cross, we understand how Count Von Zinzindorf, one of the great followers of Christ in the 1700s could say, 'I have but one passion; it is He [Jesus], He alone.'**

"As we take communion [and/or hand out nails], let's reflect on how He demonstrated His awesome love for us on the cross. Then, seriously ask Jesus this question: 'How can I love You and live for You more passionately?'"

Closing
Activity Options

Conclude by taking the Lord's Supper with students. Use this special time to further explain the death and resurrection of Jesus. Make it especially meaningful by carefully choosing appropriate background music or no music at all, subdued lighting with candles, etc.

Hand out a nail to each student. Encourage each student to keep the nail in his or her pocket, make it into a necklace or put it somewhere to serve as a reminder of what Jesus did for them.

No Equal to His Resurrection
How Can I Have That Kind of Power?

The Hook

Begin this session by saying, "**Dead fish float downstream. Only live fish swim upstream. All of us want the power to swim upstream, the power to be different. Have you noticed those commercials on TV that talk about being different and say things like 'different is good'? We all desire the strength to face the crowd and do what's right. But where do we find the strength to swim upstream?**

"**While some students lack the willpower to withstand the slightest pressure to drink a beer or take drugs, other students have learned to draw on a power that helps them stand under incredible pressures—even in the face of death. Let me introduce you to a couple of 17-year-olds who discovered that power.**"

Hero #1: Cassie Bernall

"**Cassie was a 17-year-old junior at Columbine High School in Littleton, Colorado. She was reading her Bible in the school library when a fellow student pointed his gun at her and asked, 'Do you believe in God?' She calmly responded, 'Yes, I believe in God.' Those words were her last. The gunman shot her. A classmate described the scene to Larry King on CNN: 'She completely stood up for God. When the killers asked her if there was anyone who had faith in Christ, she spoke up and they shot her for it.'**"[1]

Hero #2: Ben Strong

"**Just a year and a half before Cassie made her courageous stand, Ben experienced a similar situation. The place? Heath High School in Paducah, Kentucky. The setting? A before-school prayer meeting, where a fellow student had walked in and began shooting students. At a time when most of us would have desperately begged for mercy or scrambled behind the nearest desk, Ben Strong took a stand. He asked the killer to drop his weapon. But the gunman kept firing. So Ben walked right up to him, looking straight into his eyes, and said, 'What are you doing? Don't shoot. Just put the gun down.' Then he grabbed the gunman by the shoulders, and the weapon, which still contained a live round, dropped to the floor. The principal, who was just about to enter the room, stated that Strong almost certainly saved him from taking the next bullet.**"

After sharing these incredible examples, tell students that all of us would hopefully have that kind of courage in a similar situation. Point out that they *can* have it by taking a hard look at Jesus' resurrection.

Lead in prayer, or ask one of your more confident students to ask

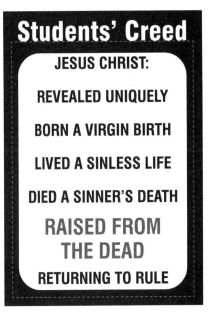

the main point

By the end of this session, students should know that because Jesus rose from the dead, they can live today in His resurrection power.

Students' Creed

JESUS CHRIST:

REVEALED UNIQUELY

BORN A VIRGIN BIRTH

LIVED A SINLESS LIFE

DIED A SINNER'S DEATH

RAISED FROM THE DEAD

RETURNING TO RULE

Preparation:

Bibles; *Passion: Better Is One Day* CD to play as students enter and exit; *Listen: Louder* CD; CD player; PowerPoint®, a transparency and an overhead projector or chalkboard and chalk.

A week before you teach this session, ask some of your students to come prepared to tell about a dramatic answer to prayer they have experienced or they know about from another source. Before the session, you will need to copy Philippians 3:10, 11 *(The Living Bible)* on an overhead transparency, the chalkboard or put it in a PowerPoint® presentation.

Play a clip of Jesus' resurrection from the *Jesus* movie or *Jesus of Nazareth*. You may want to discuss some of the false theories concerning Jesus' disappearance that are found in the *Jesus no equal* devotional.

for God's direction in this session.

Give students an opportunity to reflect on their devotions from the past week by asking:

• **How do we know that Jesus' resurrection wasn't some kind of elaborate hoax?**

(His miracles set Him apart from everyone else, but especially the miracle of His resurrection. No one on earth has ever been clinically dead for three days and lived to tell about it. Truly, there's no equal to Jesus in all of human history.)

The Message

What does the resurrection of Jesus Christ have to do with living a powerful Christian life today? Ask for a volunteer to read aloud Ephesians 1:18-20.

Then say, **"Here's a tough question: What does Paul tell the Ephesians that they need to do to get this power?"** *(Nothing. He assumes that the power resides within them as Christians. He just prays that they will realize the power that they already have.)*

• **And just how great is that power?**

(It is "incomparably great" and "mighty," like the power that raised Jesus from the dead.)

• **Is this power available only to missionaries, or to everyone?**

(See Ephesians 1:1, which was written to the saints at Ephesus, which means all Christians.)

Continue this discussion by saying, **"Many Christians haven't learned to draw on this power. Why? Let's look at some verses to find out why many students live without God's power."**

Let students read the verses prior to giving the principle. See if they can discover them first.

1. Get Jesus

Look again at Ephesians 1:19. God's "incomparably great power" isn't given to just anyone. Who is it for? *("For us who believe.")* Unbelievers, those who don't know Jesus personally, can't have this power.

Comment, **"I like the Christian bumper sticker that parodies the 'Got Milk?' advertisements. It reads, 'Got Jesus?' Those two words hold the key to a powerful, victorious life. 'Got Jesus?' It was the key for Ben and Cassie. Let's take a closer look at Cassie's life."**

Illustration

"You have to go back to Cassie's ninth-grade year to discover where she first tapped into God's resurrection power. You see, back then she lived for the dark side. She had a dark view of life, with interests that included witchcraft, drugs, drinking and suicide. When her parents found out, they took radical action, moving her to a different school, cutting her off from her

negative friends, and introducing her to a youth minister. You can imagine how excited Cassie was about that turn of events. But one day, she went on a retreat with the youth group. According to her dad, the Cassie that left for the retreat was gloomy, with her head down and nothing to say. But the Cassie that returned was a different person—her eyes bright and excited about life. Her father said, 'It was like she was in a dark room, and somebody turned the light on, and she saw the beauty that was surrounding her.' She told her mom she'd totally changed, and she'd prove it to her."

Challenge students by saying, **"Do you lack power in your life? Perhaps you're a person who admires Jesus from afar, but has never gotten to know Him personally. Or, maybe you're a lot like Cassie, who had become controlled by the power of the dark side. It wasn't too late for Cassie to turn back, and it's not too late for you."**

2. Know God

Comment, **"In the days of the Old Testament, God gave His prophet Daniel a vision of the future, a vision of a furious, evil leader waging war, corrupting people, seeking to destroy what is holy. Sounds like a nightmare, starring the Darth lords of *Star Wars*. But some people will have the power to resist the evil one. Let's read Daniel 11:32 to find out more."**

"With flattery he will corrupt those who have violated the covenant, but the people who know their God will firmly resist him."

Ask students:

• **What do you think it means to "know God"?**

Allow students to respond, then say, **"Isn't it more than just praying a prayer at a retreat, or saying grace at meal times? God is not concerned with tallying up who keeps the most rules. The Pharisees were great at keeping rules, but Jesus wasn't impressed. God primarily wants us to know Him and love Him. Love God, and the lifestyle will follow."**

Ask, **"What are some ways we can get personal with God, and get to know Him better?"** *(Talk to Him, read His Word, praise Him, etc.)*

3. Be Filled with the Spirit

Ask for a volunteer to read Ephesians 5:18, or read it from *The Message*:

"Don't drink too much wine. That cheapens your life. Drink the Spirit of God, huge draughts of him." You may also want to read Romans 8:9-11.

Then say something like this: **"When we receive Christ, the Spirit of God enters our lives. After that, we are to live a life that is controlled and empowered by the Holy Spirit."**

Play the song "Spirit," by Switchfoot, recorded on the *Listen: Louder* CD. The lyricist asks the Spirit to "fall fresh on me," "be my joy" and finds all his longings filled in Him. Tell students that the Spirit of God is waiting to do all of these things for us; He is just waiting for us to ask.

SMALL GROUP
PRAYER:

Help students get in smaller groups of two to four for this activity. Then say, **"We all have issues in our lives that we just don't have the power to deal with on our own. Maybe it's dealing with ridicule at school, pressures at home, getting along with your parents. Whatever the problem, let's get on our knees and pour out our hearts to God. If it's a private issue, then pray privately about it. But if you want your group to add their prayers, then pray aloud so they can pray with you."**

Microsoft is a registered trademark of Microsoft Corporation in the United States and/or other countries.

What does "controlled" mean?

Comment, **"If you allow dirt to enter the gas tank of your car, don't be surprised if your engine loses power and sputters. Ben and Cassie kept their gas tanks clean. In other words, they let the Spirit call the shots in their lives. Ben wasn't at the prayer meeting just because some girl he liked was going. He was the leader of the prayer meeting. Cassie was known for bringing her Bible to school every day, and for her involvement in ministering to people in one of the roughest sections of Denver. Just two days before she died, her church was putting together a video and recorded her saying these words, 'I just try to not contradict myself, to get rid of all the hypocrisy and just live for Christ.'**

"Do you want to be filled with the Spirit? First, you must allow Jesus to call the shots in your life."

What does "empowered" mean?

Continue by saying, **"The apostle Paul wrote most of the books of the New Testament and lived a life of incredible zeal and power. Where did he get the power? He talks about it in 1 Corinthians 15:10."** Have someone read the verse aloud.

"Jesus Himself said in John 15:5, '. . . *apart from me you can do nothing.'*

"Do you want to be filled with the Spirit? Realize that without Him you can't do anything. Ask Him to fill you as you wake up every morning. As He does, you will learn to stop trusting in your own abilities and strengths. You will start to trust Him for the power you need to live each day."

4. Pray for His Power

Share this story with students:

"Bill Gates is the wealthiest man in America. He's also extremely intelligent. Whenever you use Microsoft® Windows, Microsoft® Word or Microsoft® anything, you're looking at the name of his company, Microsoft Corporation. But his mind is so absorbed with the world of computers that he often overlooks the little details of life, like his gas gauge and his wallet.

"In the middle of the night in the middle of winter, Gates ran out of gas on a freeway somewhere near Microsoft's headquarters. He coasted off the side of the road, walked back to a Ramada Inn and requested a room. But when they asked for his ID and a deposit, he couldn't find his wallet. And no matter how hard he tried to convince the desk clerk that he was Bill Gates, worked down the street at Microsoft and that an assistant would pay in the morning, the skeptical clerk stood her ground. She had probably heard similar lines before. No money? No room. Probably some bum off the street. So that night, the CEO who would make around $100 million that year took a lonely walk to his office in the cold."[2]

The point of this story is that it didn't matter how much money Bill Gates had in the bank if he couldn't access it. In the same way, God's power is available for us. But we can't access it without prayer. Picture it as a credit card with the pin # JER333. That stands for Jeremiah 33:3, which says, *"Call to me and I will answer you and tell you great and unsearchable things you do not know."*

At this point, invite students you have previously contacted to share the answers they received to their prayers. Ask, **"Could some of you share any dramatic answers to prayer that you have personally experienced, or any miracles that you know of from other sources?"**

After students have finished sharing their answered prayers, say, **"It's no accident that Ben Strong had just finished praying with other believers before he made his courageous stand. And a part of Ben's prayer that morning was for strength to last through the day."**

5. Take in His Word

Have several students read aloud John 15:7 and Hebrews 4:12.

"But if you make yourselves at home with me and my words are at home in you, you can be sure that whatever you ask will be listened to and acted upon" (John 15:7, *The Message*).

Ask students, **"Do you know what Cassie Bernall was doing in the library when the killer entered? She was reading her Bible—no big shock to anyone who knew her. You see, she brought her Bible with her to school almost every day. I think Cassie's mind was filled with the power and perspective of God's Word. She knew that her earthly life was just a vapor, and after the vapor vanished, she would be in Heaven for all eternity. That's how she could tell her mom not long before the shooting: 'Mom, it would be OK if I died. I'd be in a better place, and you know where I'd be.'**

"I don't want to give the impression that God's resurrection power necessarily makes us into Jedi Knights that wow everyone with their power. The apostle Paul found that God had no intention of taking away one of his weaknesses. But God's power was perfected through that weakness. (See 2 Corinthians 12:7-10.) And sometimes His power is even perfected through death.

"I don't pretend to know all the reasons why God allowed Cassie to die so young. But I can tell you that by her courageous stand in her death, she probably inspired more people than she ever could have through her life. The press releases went worldwide. And at her memorial service, over 75 students indicated that they made first-time commitments to Christ. What an impact!"

A song on the *Listen: Louder CD* reminds us of Cassie's life. Play the song "Hallelujah," by the Newsboys, and ask students to list qualities that characterized her life. These qualities are evidence of resurrection power!

The Application

Before the session, you will need to copy Philippians 3:10, 11 *(The Living Bible)* on an overhead transparency, the chalkboard or put it in a PowerPoint® presentation.

To conclude the session, ask students: **"Do you want to begin the road to experiencing the incredible power that fueled both Cassie's and Ben's heroic stands? If so, I want to give you the opportunity to read in unison a commitment to die to self and live unreservedly for Christ. This is a passage that the apostle Paul wrote 2000 years ago. It meant so much to Cassie that she wrote it out word for word just two days before her death. I'll give you a chance to read it silently first, to see if you're willing to say it out loud. Don't feel pressured. This is heavy stuff, and you may need some time to think about it. Let's read it as a prayer to God."**

"Now I have given up everything else
I have found it to be the only way
To really know Christ and to experience
The mighty power that brought
Him back to life again, and to find
Out what it means to suffer and to
Die with him. So, whatever it takes
I will be one who lives in the fresh
Newness of life of those who are
Alive from the dead" (Philippians 3:10, 11, TLB).

No Equal to His Lordship
What Should I Do Until Jesus Returns?

The Hook

Begin this session by saying, **"Anyone who has seen the *Star Wars* series or the *Indiana Jones* trilogy knows the incredible excitement that producer George Lucas can pack into a movie. But it's doubtful that Lucas would have made anything at all of his life, had he not first given up his old dreams. During his teenage years, a lot of people considered him a loser who was going nowhere in life. He never applied himself in school and dreamed only about racing cars. But his dreams all ended just a few days before his graduation. While driving home from the library in his Fiat, he prepared for a left turn by glancing in his rearview mirror. But, as he started the turn, he heard the sound of another car, a blowing horn and the impact of a speeding Chevy crunching into the driver side of his car. It should have killed him. The little Fiat turned four or five complete flips before it wrapped around a solid oak tree. The impact was so great that it actually moved the entire tree a couple of feet over, leaving a huge hole in its former position.**

"Miraculously, George survived. Get this: during the Fiat's third flip, his regulation racing seat belt snapped, throwing him out of the open top and onto the ground. He was close to death, but recovered slowly through two weeks in the hospital and months of physical therapy. His Fiat didn't survive, ending up in the junkyard.

"After the accident, George Lucas was a changed person. He decided there must be some reason he survived, and set his mind to get his act together and make something out of his life. He left his racing dreams behind and decided to go to college. There, he developed an interest in literature and writing. And instead of *driving* race cars, he began *filming* them. Today, he's glad for his decision to let his old life and his old dreams die, so that he could go a new direction. Without giving up his old life, he would have never found his niche in the film industry, and no one would have ever seen *Star Wars*."[1]

The point of the opening illustration is this: Many students—and adults as well—are unwilling to totally give their lives to Christ, because they're afraid of what they will have to give up. So they never let go of their old lives. Today you will challenge your students to hold those areas of their lives with an open hand and look at them carefully. Are they holding them back from a life that they never dreamed possible?

Open with prayer or ask one of your students to thank God for all He has been teaching them in this study of the life of Christ.

the main point

By the end of this session, students should give their lives unreservedly to Jesus and sign the Challenge 2000 Covenant.

Students' Creed

JESUS CHRIST:

REVEALED UNIQUELY

BORN A VIRGIN BIRTH

LIVED A SINLESS LIFE

DIED A SINNER'S DEATH

RAISED FROM THE DEAD

RETURNING TO RULE

Preparation:
Bibles; *Passion: Better Is One Day* CD to play as students enter and exit; *Listen: Louder* CD; CD player; transparency and overhead projector or chalk and chalkboard; reproducible Challenge 2000 Covenant on page 9 of this book; blank paper for each student; writing utensils

Show a clip from *The Last Crusade* (the final movie of the *Indiana Jones* trilogy). After the explorers find the Holy Grail, they are trying to escape the cave before everything falls apart. A girl dies while trying to retrieve the cup, then Indy tries to recover it from a ledge that he can almost reach. But his father realizes that Indy will lose his life trying to get the cup. He looks at him and says, "Indy, give it up." You can tell that Indy wants the cup more than anything, but finally he gives up the cup and saves his own life. There are some things we desperately want to hold on to, but God knows they will kill us. God is pleading with us, "Give it up."

SMALL GROUP DISCUSSION: ____

Divide students into groups of five or less for this activity. Ask them to talk about some reasons why many people today refuse to submit to the lordship of Christ. What holds them back from totally giving their lives to Jesus? Give them sufficient time, then ask students to appoint someone from their group to report their answers to everyone else.

The Message

Comment, **"It's hard to believe that this session wraps up our series on *Jesus no equal*. Let's take a moment to reflect on where we've been. We've seen that compared to Jesus there is:**
  * *No Equal to His Claims*
  * *No Equal to His Humility*
  * *No Equal to His Servanthood*
  * *No Equal to His Sacrifice*
  * *No Equal to His Resurrection*

"Today, we move past His resurrection to see what He's up to now. We looked at some verses in Philippians several weeks ago, when we saw how Jesus humbled Himself by coming from Heaven to earth to live as a servant and die as a criminal. In the words of radio commentator Paul Harvey, 'This is the rest of the story.'"

Ask for a volunteer to read aloud Philippians 2:9-11.

Afterward, say, **"These verses tell us that when we understand the exalted Jesus in all His glory, there is *No Equal to His Lordship*. Jesus is worthy of our worship and our allegiance. He's worthy to be our Lord, the one who leads our lives. Jesus' first-century followers understood this. That's why they set aside their own hopes and dreams in order to embrace God's hopes and dreams for their lives.**

"Here are some reasons that people, and probably some of us here, hesitate to give Jesus full control of our lives."

1. *"I'm still not convinced that it's all true."*

"Some of you may be thinking, 'Well, I've still got my doubts about whether this whole Jesus thing is true or not.' If this is what's holding you back, even after reading all the evidence presented in *Jesus no equal*, I've got a challenge for you: Explain why Jesus' disciples died for a lie.

"If anyone would have known that the resurrection was a hoax, it was Jesus' disciples. Remember, they claimed to have talked with Him and eaten with Him after He rose. They said that they touched His resurrected body, and they confirmed the nail prints in His hands."

Ask your students to imagine for a moment that they are some of the disciples following the cruel death of their Master. Imagine that Jesus never rose from the dead. If they were to identify themselves with Jesus, they could be the next prospects to hang on a cross. So what would they do? They would probably lay low about the Jesus stuff. They'd go back to their families and try to put their lives back together.

In this scenario they would have no reason to concoct some wild story about Jesus rising from the dead. And they'd be crazy to dedicate the rest of their lives to spreading a lie that they knew would snuff out every other dream they had for their lives and exchange it for suffering, imprisonment and the likelihood of a painful execution.

Continue by saying, **"Some men of history have died for ideas that were untrue. But martyrs for a cause believe that their ideas are true. If Jesus' resurrection and miracles did not happen, then, of all people, the disciples knew they didn't happen. It would be incredible to believe that they gave up their lives for something they knew was a lie."**

Ask students, **"From your devotions this past week, do you remember how each of Jesus' disciples died? History tells us how much these guys believed that Jesus was Lord."**

- Andrew: *death by crucifixion*
- Bartholomew: *death by crucifixion*
- James, the brother of Jesus: *death by stoning*
- James, the son of Alphaeus: *death by crucifixion*
- James, the son of Zebedee: *death by the sword*
- John: *although banished to a small island in his later years, perhaps sentenced to hard labor in the quarries, he may have died a natural death*
- Matthew: *death by the sword*
- Peter: *death by crucifixion (upside down)*
- Philip: *death by crucifixion*
- Simon: *death by crucifixion*
- Thaddaeus: *death by arrows*
- Thomas: *death by a spear*

Comment, **"If you're still not sure that Jesus worked the miracles He worked and rose from the dead, then you've got some pretty tough explaining to do. Why did all these people die for something that they knew was a lie?"**

2. "I'm afraid Jesus will mess up my life."

Say something like this: **"For most people, the real issue is not that they have sincere doubts. Jesus has the solution for sincere doubters. He says, 'Seek and you shall find.' Sincere seekers ask questions, trying to get answers any way they can. The real block to submitting to the lordship of Christ is that people don't want Jesus interfering with their lives. Aldous Huxley was a guy who was known for writing and lecturing against Christianity. Listen to what he wrote:**

'I had motives for not wanting the world to have a meaning. . . . For myself, no doubt, for most of my contemporaries, the philosophy of meaninglessness was essentially an instrument of liberation from . . . a certain system of morality because it interfered with our sexual freedom.'[2]

"So, if intellectual doubts aren't your problem, then the problem may be that you are afraid Jesus will mess up your life. Isn't that the real issue? We're afraid that if we give our lives completely to Jesus, He'll make us give up a friend we like, hang around the

ILLUSTRATION:

When a university student shared his faith with a fellow student, he replied, "Oh, I used to go to church and all, but now I have these intellectual problems with Christianity." To see if this was the real issue, the Christian asked, "Tell me, if I could convince you that Jesus worked the miracles He worked, rose from the dead, and was indeed the Son of God, would you be willing to give Him your life?" The student kind of smiled and said, "Well . . . I guess that's really the problem. I just don't want to give up my partying."

house and do chores all the time, watch religious television and become a missionary to Pygmies."

Continue this discussion by asking students what they would say to those who are afraid God will mess up their lives. As they share their responses, have someone record them on a transparency or the chalkboard.

Some of their responses may include these:

• *People who fear that God will mess up their lives have misunderstood God's heart. He loves them.*

Romans 5:8 says, *"But God put his love on the line for us by offering his Son in sacrificial death while we were of no use whatever to him" (The Message).*

"Once we understand how much God loves us, we can move beyond our fear and make that commitment."

• *God wants what's best for everyone.*

Jesus said in Matthew 7:11: *"If you, then, though you are evil, know how to give good gifts to your children, how much more will your Father in heaven give good gifts to those who ask him!"*

"One student declared when he finally understood this, 'What am I doing fooling around outside of God's will and missing out on God's best for my life?'"

• *Being one's own boss is an illusion.*

In 1 John 5:19, we find these words: *"We know that we are children of God, and that the whole world is under the control of the evil one."*

"People who don't want to submit to Jesus would rather call their own shots. What they don't understand is that nobody completely calls his own shots. You've got to serve somebody. If you're not a slave to God, you're a slave to sin. If God is not in control, then Satan is. And just as God has a plan for your life, so does Satan. Here are the two plans. God gives you the freedom to choose the one you want."

• **Plan A: Satan's Plan for Your Life**

"Your enemy the devil prowls around like a roaring lion looking for someone to devour" (1 Peter 5:8).

• **Plan B: Jesus' Plan for Your Life**

"I came so they can have real and eternal life, more and better life than they ever dreamed of" (John 10:10, *The Message*).

"There's no plan 'C.' Do you want to choose 'A' or 'B'?"

• *Our side wins.*

Jesus didn't sugarcoat the Christian life. He spoke clearly to His disciples: *"If they persecuted me, they will persecute you also"* (John 15:20). *"In this world you will have trouble. But take heart! I have overcome the world"* (John 16:33).

"Let's shoot straight. There will be sacrifice. God may ask you to give up some things that are dear to you. You may be called on to give up your life for Him. But it's worth it. To be sure, Satan wreaks a lot of havoc in the world today. Often, it looks like his

team is winning. But that's temporary. The book of Revelation is complex in many ways, but the main point is crystal clear: *our side wins!* Sometimes Christians look like the losers. But God never said that it would appear that we were ahead at halftime. It's enough to know that we're on the winning team. And in the end, everyone will acknowledge that Jesus is Lord."

The Application

Introduce the closing section of this study by saying something like this: **"For six weeks, we've seen that there is no equal to Jesus. No one else even comes close. Look through human history, and you'll find lots of men who wanted to become gods. But only one God wanted to become a man. It's time to take the first step, to make the next decision."**

As you ask these questions, allow time for them to sink in:

• **Do you think Jesus deserves your allegiance?**
• **Are you ready to give Him total control of your life?**
• **Are you prepared to give Him that one area that you keep holding on to?**
• **Are you ready to pursue Him and all that He wants for you?**

Distribute two pieces of paper to each student, one is blank and the other is the Challenge 2000 Covenant on page 9. Continue by saying, **"No one will see these papers but you. As I have said each week, the Challenge 2000 Covenant has been signed by thousands of students nationwide, who are sold out to Jesus, and have committed themselves to take His message to every student in their school. By signing this, you join with this national movement of students who are out to change their world.**

"Let's look closely at each part of the covenant, to make sure your heart is in it before you sign it. As I read and explain each part, ask the Holy Spirit to reveal your attitudes and actions that are inconsistent with the covenant. If you discover anything that would keep you from living out the covenant, write it on the blank piece of paper. Don't sign it—it's between you and God."

Read through and explain each part of the Covenant. Then ask, **"Are you willing to give up whatever holds you back from signing this covenant? If so, sign the Challenge 2000 Covenant."**

Instruct students to form a line and come to the front of the room. Their first stop will be a trash can, into which they will tear up and throw away the paper on which they wrote their inconsistencies. Encourage them to pray this prayer: **"Lord, I can't overcome what's on this paper, but You can! Release the power of Your Spirit on me."** The second stop will be a table, where they can deposit their Challenge 2000 Covenant.

Conclude, **"We all serve somebody, either ourselves, the evil one or Jesus. There is no in-between. No compromise. I hope that this series has convinced you that there's *no equal* to Jesus!"**

MUSIC SUGGESTION:

As students complete the Challenge 2000 Covenant and drop them on the table, play the song "Omega," recorded by Rebecca St. James on the *Listen: Louder* CD. This song is a great benediction to this study. May the amazing grace of our Master go with your students!

Session 1

[1]Used by permission of Dave Tippett.
[2]*History and Christianity* by John Warwick Montgomery, 1964, InterVarsity Press, Downers Grove, IL.
[3]*Mere Christianity* by C. S. Lewis, 1960, The MacMillan Co., New York, NY. Used by permission.

Session 3

[1]*Entertainment Weekly*, January 10, 1997.
[2]*Arnold: The Education of a Bodybuilder* by Arnold Schwarzenegger and Douglas Kent Hall, 1977, New York. Reprinted with permission of Simon and Schuster, Inc.

Session 4

[1]"SNL Alum's Death Echoes Belushi's," *The Atlanta Journal and Constitution* by Lyle V. Harris, December 19, 1997.
[2]Facts from *Companion to the Baptist Hymnal* by William J. Reynolds, 1976, Broadman Press, Nashville, TN.

Session 5

[1]"Littleton's Martyrs," "Breakpoint Commentary," Charles W. Colson, April 26, 1999.
[2]Facts gathered from *Gates* by Stephen Manes and Paul Andrews, 1993, 1994, Simon and Schuster, New York.

Session 6

[1]*Skywalking: The Life and Films of George Lucas* by Dale Pollock, 1983, Harmony Books.
[2]*Tell It Often, Tell It Well* by Mark McCloskey, 1985, Here's Life Publishers, Inc., San Bernadino, CA.

about the authors

Barry St. Clair

Barry St. Clair's primary desire is to see spiritual awakening take place in the younger genera-tion. As the founder and president of Reach Out Youth Solutions in Atlanta, Georgia, he has immersed himself in youth ministry for over thirty years. Barry speaks to and equips thousands of students and youth workers every year, both in the United States and around the world. Barry has authored over twenty books. He played on the number three basketball team in the nation, and has run the Boston Marathon. Barry lives in Atlanta, Georgia, and has six children.

Steve Miller

As a high school student, Steve Miller met Jesus and has never gotten over it. For the past 25 years he has ministered to students and leaders of students through local churches and campus ministries. He lived in Slovakia as a youth worker trainer and currently writes both national and international online youth worker resources for Reach Out Youth Solutions at www.reach-out.org. He authored *The Contemporary Christian Music Debate*. Steve lives in Acworth, Georgia, and has four children.

"I remember when I first got saved. It was such a life-changing experience that for days, for weeks, for months all I could talk about was Jesus. It seemed like everything in some way was connected to Him. And if it wasn't, it didn't hold my attention for long. I even remember friends ask-ing me, 'Man, how did you get from talking about football, or what was on TV to talking about Jesus? Is that all you think about?' Those were the days! In his book, *Jesus no equal*, Barry St. Clair successfully helps us reclaim that fiery love and adoration for God by the most effective way known to man—simply by fixing our eyes on the one and only Jesus with whom there is no equal. When I read the book, I was moved. He creatively and consistently kept pointing back to Jesus, and that's exactly what I needed. Whether you're a new babe in Christ or a seasoned saint, get ready to be awed, greeted, challenged and changed by the one and only Jesus no equal."
Fred D. Lynch III
Urban Ministry Coordinator
Josh McDowell Ministries

"It's time for a super revolution and young people all over are getting serious about Jesus. This book will help them get captured with a passion for the Lord."
Ron Luce
President/CEO, *Teen Mania Ministries*

"Today in our generation, the young people are dealing with a lot of hurt and tragedy all around them. They are desperately crying out for answers to the life they face every day. The timing of Barry's book, *Jesus no equal*, is perfect. It not only helps those young people who know Jesus to grow in their understanding of how Jesus works in their everyday life, it also gives them tools by which they can share Jesus with the lost and hurting generation . . . their generation."
Mark Price
Former NBA All-star

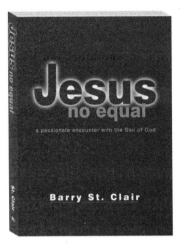